Letters (
-et, -

MW00743554

SCHOOL PUBLISHERS

Photos:
p.2, net © Veer; p. 3, leg © Harcourt Telescope ; p. 4, pen © Harcourt Telescope; p. 5, © Shutterstock; p. 6, © Shutterstock; p. 7, © Harcourt Telescope; p. 8, © Harcourt Telescope.

Printed in China

ISBN 10: 0-15-358381-9
ISBN 13: 978-0-15-358381-0

Ordering Options
ISBN 10: 0-15-358355-X (Grade K Below-Level Collection)
ISBN 13: 978-0-15-358355-1 (Grade K Below-Level Collection)
ISBN 10: 0-15-360634-7 (package of 5)
ISBN 13: 978-0-15-360634-2 (package of 5)

11 12 13 14 15 0940 15 14 13 12 11 10

net

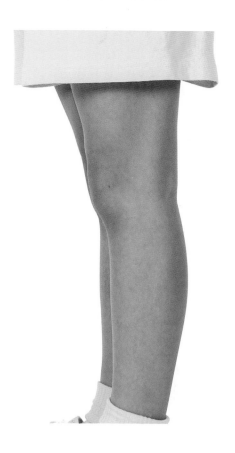

leg

pen

hen

jet

ten

wet